Y0-CZQ-013

Family Fun

Learning the F Sound

Greg Moskal

Phonics
for the
REAL World™

Rosen Classroom Books and Materials™
New York

Big families have fun.

3

Small families have fun.

5

Families play football.

Families play with pets.

9

Families go for bike rides.

Families go fishing.

Families grow plants.

Families fix dinner.

Families eat fun foods.

19

Families have fun!

Word List

families
fishing
fix
foods
football
for
fun

Instructional Guide

One of the essential skills that enable a young child to read is the ability to associate letter-sound symbols and blend these sounds to form words. Phonics instruction can teach children a system that will help them decode unfamiliar words and, in turn, enhance their word-recognition skills. We offer a phonics-based series of books that are easy to read and understand. Each book pairs words and pictures that reinforce specific phonetic sounds in a logical sequence. Topics are based on curriculum goals appropriate for early readers in the areas of science, social studies, and health.

Letter/Sound: **f** – Write the familiar number words *four* and *five* on a chalkboard or dry-erase board. Ask the child how the words are alike and how they are different. Ask the following questions: "Which word names the number of letters it has?" "Which word has fewer letters than it names?" Have the child underline the initial consonant **f** in each word. Have the child name a word that begins with **f** and means the opposite of *near (far)*. Continue with the following opposites: *slow – fast, lose – find, many – few, to – from, real – fake*. List the words that have initial consonant **f**. Have the child underline the initial consonant in each word. Have them suggest additions to the list of initial consonant **f** words.

Phonics Activities: Provide work sheets containing pictures of items with initial consonants **m**, **t**, **b**, **f**. Have the child name each picture and write the correct consonant beneath it.
- Duplicate several sets of playing cards with line drawings of familiar items with initial **m**, **t**, **b**, **f** (at least 24 cards in each set). Have two people or a group of children play "Go Fish" with this deck of cards.
- Have the child complete unfinished oral sentences with appropriate initial **f** words. (Example: *Clowns make us laugh because they're* _____ *[funny]*). List the child's responses on the chalkboard or dry-erase board. Have them underline the initial consonant **f** in each word.

Additional Resources:
- Hausherr, Rosemarie. *Celebrating Families*. New York: Scholastic, Inc., 1997.
- MacGregor, Cynthia. *Creative Family Projects: Exciting & Practical Activities You Can Do Together*. Secaucus, NJ: Carol Publishing Group, 1995.
- Sweeney, Joan. *Me & My Family Tree*. New York: Crown Books for Young Readers, 2000.

Published in 2002 by The Rosen Publishing Group, Inc.
29 East 21st Street, New York, NY 10010

Copyright © 2002 by The Rosen Publishing Group, Inc.

All rights reserved. No part of this book may be reproduced in any form without permission in writing from the publisher, except by a reviewer.

Book Design: Ron A. Churley

Photo Credits: Cover, p. 17 © Bob Schatz/International Stock; pp. 3, 5, 7, 9, 11, 15, 19 © SuperStock; p. 13 © Scott Barrow/International Stock; p. 21 © Peter Langone/International Stock.

Library of Congress Cataloging-in-Publication Data

Moskal, Greg, 1971-
  Family fun: learning the F sound / author, Greg Moskal.— 1st ed.
     p. cm. — (Power phonics/phonics for the real world)
  ISBN 0-8239-5901-5 (lib. bdg.)
  ISBN 0-8239-8246-7 (pbk.)
  6-pack ISBN 0-8239-9214-4
  1. Family recreation—Juvenile literature. [1. Family life.]
I. Title. II. Series.
  GV182.8 .M67 2002
  790.1'91—dc21
                                        00-013080

Manufactured in the United States of America